Stand Out B

Reading & Writing Challenge

Rob Jenkins • Staci Sabbagh Johnson

Australia • Canada • Mexico • Singapore • Spain • United Kingdom • United States

Stand Out Basic

Reading & Writing Challenge

Rob Jenkins • Staci Sabbagh Johnson

Publisher, Adult and Academic ESL: *James W. Brown*
Senior Acquisitions Editor: *Sherrise Roehr*
Director of Product Development: *Anita Raducanu*
Development Editor: *Tom Jefferies*
Editorial Assistant: *Katherine Reilly*
Director of Product Marketing: *Amy Mabley*
Senior Field Marketing Manager: *Donna Lee Kennedy*
Product Marketing Manager: *Laura Needham*
Senior Production Editor: *Maryellen Killeen*
Senior Manufacturing Coordinator: *Mary Beth Hennebury*
Photo Researcher: *Melissa Goodrum*
Project Manager: *Tünde A. Dewey*
Compositor: *Pre-Press Company, Inc.*
Printer: *West Group*
Cover Designer: *Rotunda Design*
Illustrators: *Ray Medici*
James Edwards, represented by Sheryl Beranbaum
Scott MacNeill

Printed in the United States of America.

3 4 5 6 7 8 9 10 09 08 07

For more information, contact Thomson Heinle, 25 Thomson Place, Boston, MA 02210 USA, or you can visit our Internet site at elt.thomson.com

Library of Congress Control Number 2005928923
ISBN-13: 978-1-4130-0720-6
ISBN-10: 1-4130-0720-1
International Student Edition ISBN: 1-4130-2092-5

CONTENTS

TO THE TEACHER

About *Stand Out: Standards-Based Learning*

The ***Stand Out*** series includes a five-level basal series for English language learners designed to facilitate active learning, while challenging students to build a nurturing and effective learning community.

About *Stand Out Reading & Writing Challenge*

Stand Out Reading & Writing Challenge was written to give students additional practice in vocabulary, reading, and writing, while focusing students' attention on life-skill content.

Stand Out Reading & Writing Challenge is aligned with the basal series and is divided into eight distinct units, mirroring competency areas most useful to newcomers. These areas are outlined in CASAS assessment programs and different state model standards for adults.

No prior content knowledge is required to use ***Stand Out Reading & Writing Challenge.*** However, students will need the skill background necessary for their particular level. The books can be used as a supplemental component to ***Stand Out*** or as a stand-alone text.

Philosophy of *Stand Out Reading & Writing Challenge*

Stand Out Reading & Writing Challenge is intended for English language learners who need more practice with vocabulary, reading, and writing than they are given in most basal texts. Each unit takes students from a life-skill activity to vocabulary and reading practice and eventually to a finished piece of writing with the philosophy that students learn best when actively engaged in activities that relate to their personal lives and move from what they already know to new information.

Organization of *Stand Out Reading & Writing Challenge*

Stand Out Reading & Writing Challenge challenges students to develop their vocabulary, reading, and writing skills through eight unique units. Each unit includes a mix of activity types and caters to students with different learning styles.

▶ **Life-Skill Activity** Each unit opens with a life-skill activity designed to activate students' prior knowledge about the topic and prepare them for the following activities.

▶ **Vocabulary** Students are introduced to vocabulary that they need to better understand the reading. They will go through a series of activities designed to make them more familiar with the vocabulary and how it will be used. The lower levels use a variety of pictures to demonstrate much of the vocabulary. The higher levels introduce dictionary skills to help students become more independent learners.

▶ **Life-Skill Readings** Students will prepare for the reading by assessing their own knowledge and by making predictions about what they will read. Following the reading, they will do a variety of comprehension activities as well as expansion activities designed to help them relate the reading to their own lives.

▶ **Writing Practice** Students read a writing model and work through a series of pre-writing activities designed to facilitate their writing process. Their final task is to compose an original writing based on the previous model. Through the series, students progress from writing simple sentences to producing to complex paragraphs, and finally multi-paragraph writings.

▶ **Editing** Students self-correct their own work and then share with peers for more suggestions. Students complete each unit by writing a final draft.

▶ **Community Challenge** Each unit ends with a challenge that requires students to complete a community task related to the life-skill topic from the competency area that they have just worked with.

ACKNOWLEDGMENTS

The author and publisher would like to thank the following reviewers:

Marti Estrin
Santa Rosa Junior College, Santa Rosa, CA

Lawrence Fish
Shorefront YM-YWHA English Learning Program, Brooklyn, NY

Kathleen Flynn
Glendale Community College, Glendale, CA

Kathleen Jimenez
Miami-Dade Community College, Miami, FL

Daniel Loos
Seattle Central Community College, Seattle, WA

Maiyra Redman
Miami-Dade Community College, Miami, FL

Eric Rosenberg
Bronx Community College, New York, NY

PHOTO CREDIT

Unit 1
Page 3, left: ©Digital Vision/PictureQuest
Page 3, middle: ©Michael Newman/PhotoEdit
Page 3, right: ©Mark Richards/PhotoEdit
Page 4, top: ©Digital Vision/PictureQuest
Page 4, bottom: ©Mark Richards/PhotoEdit
Page 6: ©Bill Aron/PhotoEdit
Page 8: ©Bill Aron/PhotoEdit

Unit 2
Page 17: ©Amy Etra/PhotoEdit
Page 18, top: ©Amy Etra/PhotoEdit
Page 18, bottom: ©Dan Bigelow/Image Bank/Getty Images
Page 19: ©Dan Bigelow/Image Bank/Getty Images
Page 20, top: ©Amy Etra/PhotoEdit
Page 20, bottom: ©Dan Bigelow/Image Bank/Getty Images

Unit 3
Page 27, bottom all: © Hemera Photo Objects
Page 28, (ice cream): © Hemera Photo Objects
Page 29: ©David Katzenstein/CORBIS
Page 30, top: ©David Katzenstein/CORBIS
Page 30, bottom: ©Amy Etra/PhotoEdit
Page 31, left: ©David Katzenstein/CORBIS
Page 30, right: ©Amy Etra/PhotoEdit
Page 32: ©Amy Etra/PhotoEdit

Unit 5
Page 51, (bicycle): ©Hemera Photo Objects
Page 52, (bicycle): ©Hemera Photo Objects
Page 54: ©Michael Newman/PictureQuest
Page 55, top: ©Michael Newman/Picture
Page 55, bottom: ©David Katzenstein/CORBIS
Page 56: ©David Katzenstein/CORBIS

Unit 6
Page 66: ©Mary Kate Demy/Photo Edit
Page 67, top: ©Mark Anderson/Rubberball/Alamy
Page 67, bottom: ©Jim Cummins/CORBIS
Page 68: ©Jim Cummins/CORBIS

Unit 7
Page 75: ©Digital Vision/Getty Images

All *unlisted* images credit to: ©IndexOpen.com

UNIT 1 Personal Information

▶ GETTING READY

A **Look at the picture.**

B **Read.**

Amal:	Chinh, this is Matsu Tanaka. Matsu, this is Chinh.
Chinh:	Nice to meet you, Matsu.
Matsu:	Nice to meet you too, Chinh.

C **Practice Exercise B with a partner.**

▶ READING CHALLENGE 1

A **Write.**

1. Your name: ______________________
2. Your school: ______________________

B **Read.**

Jefferson College			
Last name *Moncivais*	First name *Leticia*	Birth date *April 21, 1954*	Birthplace *Mexico*
Street address *2398 South Winston Ave.*			
City *Pittsburgh*		State *Pennsylvania*	Zip *15233*
Phone *999-555-7865*		E-mail address *Lmoncivais3@email.com*	

C **Write.**

1. Name: *Leticia Moncivais*
2. School: ______________________
3. Birthplace: ______________________
4. Phone: ______________________

VOCABULARY CHALLENGE

A **Read.**

First name: Nam
Last name: Nguyen
Age: 58 years old
Marital status: Married
Birthplace: Vietnam
Phone: (714) 555-3675
School: Jolapa Adult School

First name: Eva
Last name: Malinska
Age: 60 years old
Marital status: Divorced
Birthplace: Poland
Phone: (714) 555-2121
School: Jolapa Adult School

First name: Gabriela
Last name: Ramirez
Age: 26 years old
Marital status: Single
Birthplace: Argentina
Phone: (714) 555-1218
School: Jolapa Adult School

Name
His first name is Nam.
His last name is Nguyen.

Age
Gabriela is 26 years old.

Marital status
Nam is married.
Eva is divorced.
Gabriela is single.

single

divorced

married

Birthplace
His birthplace is Vietnam.
He is from Vietnam.

School
Eva goes to Jolapa Adult School.

B Write.

1. His f_ _ _ _ _ n_ _ _ _ is Nam.
2. He is 58 y_ _ _ _ _ o_ _ _.
3. He is m_ _ _ _ _ _ _ _.
4. He is f_ _ _ _ Vietnam.
5. He goes to Jolapa Adult S_ _ _ _ _ _.

C Write.

1. Her n_ _ _ _ is Gabriela Ramirez.
2. She is 26 y_ _ _ _ _ o_ _ _.
3. She is s_ _ _ _ _ _ _.
4. Her p_ _ _ _ _ n_ _ _ _ _ _ _ is (714) 555-1218
5. She goes to Jolapa Adult S_ _ _ _ _ _.

D Circle.

1. Eva is married / divorced.
2. Eva and Gabriela are students / teachers.
3. Nam is from Argentina / Vietnam.
4. Eva is 60 / 58 years old.
5. Nam's first / last name is Nguyen.

▶ READING CHALLENGE 2

▶ PRE-READING

A **Read.**

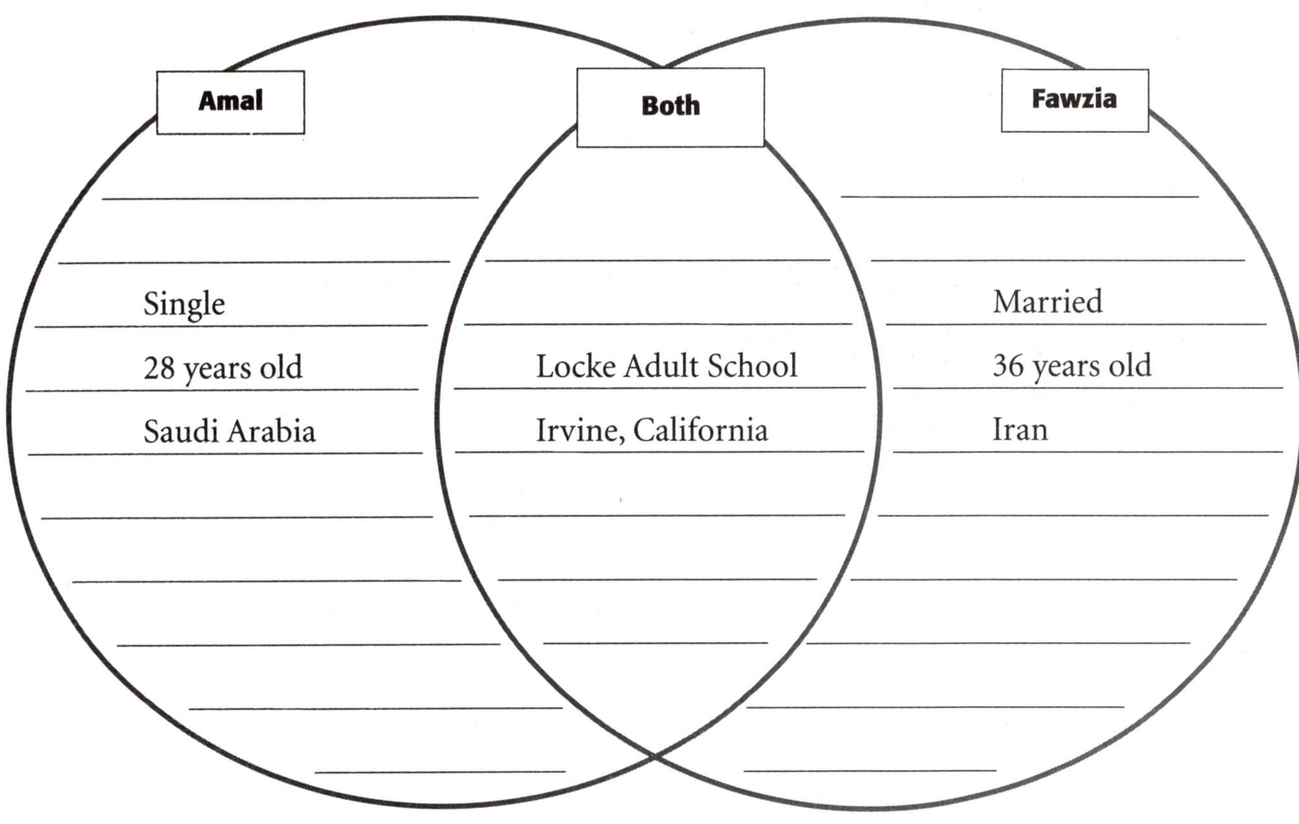

B **Circle *Yes* or *No*.**

1. Is Amal married? Yes (No)
2. Do they go to Locke Adult School? Yes No
3. Is Amal 36 years old? Yes No
4. Does Fawzia live in Irvine? Yes No
5. Is Fawzia married? Yes No

▶ READING

C **Read.**

My Story

My name is Amal Jahshan. I am 28 years old. I am from Saudi Arabia. My address is 32 Cherry Road. I live in Irvine, California. I am a student at Locke Adult School. I am single.

D **Read.**

Fawzia's Story

This is Fawzia Ahadi. She is my friend. She is 36 years old. She is from Iran. Her address is 2687 Westpark Lane. She lives in Irvine, California. She is a student at Locke Adult School. She is married.

▶ COMPRESSION

E **Write.**

Locke Adult School Application			
Last name *Jahshan*	First name		Age
Street address			Birthplace
City	State		

Locke Adult School Application			
Last name *Ahadi*	First name		Age
Street address			Birthplace
City	State		

F Write.

1. His name is ______________________.
2. He is from ______________________.
3. He is ______________________ years old.
4. He lives in ______________________.
5. He is ______________________ (single, married, divorced).
6. He goes to ______________________.

G Write.

1. Her name is ______________________.
2. She is from ______________________.
3. She is ______________________ years old.
4. She lives in ______________________.
5. She is ______________________ (single, married, divorced).
6. She goes to ______________________.

▶ EXTENSION

H Talk about the people in this unit.

A: Where is Amal from?

B: He is from Saudi Arabia.

▶ WRITING CHALLENGE

▶ PREPARING

A **Write.**

<table>
<tr><th colspan="3">School Name: ____________</th></tr>
<tr><td><u>Your</u> Last name</td><td>First name</td><td>Age</td></tr>
<tr><td colspan="2">Street address</td><td>Birthplace</td></tr>
<tr><td>City</td><td>State</td><td>Zip</td></tr>
<tr><td>Phone</td><td colspan="2">E-mail address</td></tr>
</table>

B **Copy a partner's information.**

<table>
<tr><th colspan="3">School Name: ____________</th></tr>
<tr><td><u>Partner's</u> Last name</td><td>First name</td><td>Age</td></tr>
<tr><td colspan="2">Street address</td><td>Birthplace</td></tr>
<tr><td>City</td><td>State</td><td>Zip</td></tr>
<tr><td>Phone</td><td colspan="2">E-mail address</td></tr>
</table>

C Answer the questions.

I **live** at (address).
They **live** at (address).

He **lives** at (address).
She **lives** at (address).

1. What is your name?

   My name is ______________________________.

2. Where are you from?

   I am from ______________________________.

3. How old are you?

   I am ______________________________ years old.

4. What is your address?

   I live at ______________________________.

5. Are you married?

   I am ______________________________ (single, married, divorced).

6. Where do you go to school?

   I go to ______________________________.

▶ WRITING

D Write your story.

Capital letter — Period

My name is ______________________________. I am ________ years old.
My birthplace is ______________________________. I live in ______________________________.
I am a student at ______________________________. I'm ______________________________.

E Write again.

	My Story	

▶ EDITING

F Check your writing.

- Capital letters: (M)y name is (J)ames. ~~m~~y name is ~~j~~ames.
- Periods: I am a student(.)

G Check a partner's writing.

- Capital letters: (M)y name is (J)ames. ~~m~~y name is ~~j~~ames.
- Periods: I am a student(.)

H Rewrite your story on another sheet of paper.

A **Ask people in your community these questions.**

1. What is your name?
2. Where are you from?
3. How old are you?
4. What is your address?
5. Are you married?
6. Where do you go to school?

B **Write about someone in your community.**

	______________'s Story	

C **Tell your class about the person in Exercise B.**

UNIT 2 Our Class

▶ GETTING READY

A **Look at the picture.**

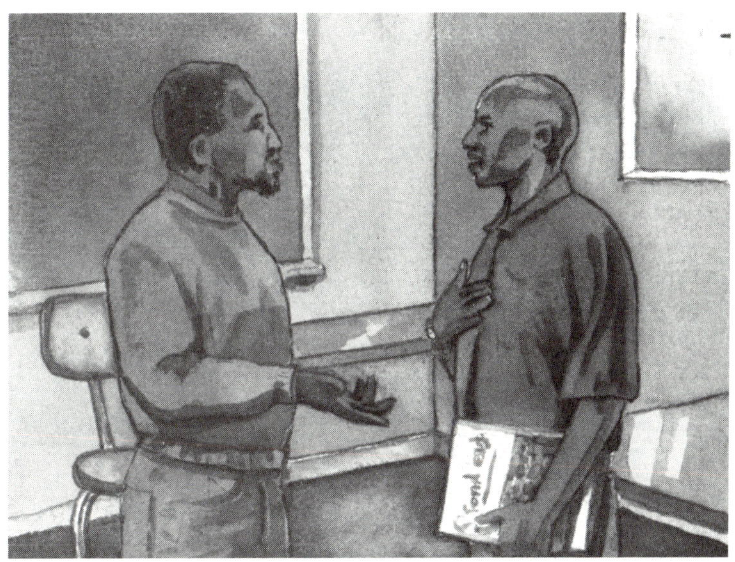

B **Read.**

Edgar:	Do you go to school?
Ron:	Yes, I go to Fort Lauderdale Adult School.
Edgar:	I do, too. What time do you go?
Ron:	I go at 9:00 A.M. on Monday and Wednesday. And you?
Edgar:	I go at 5:00 P.M. on Tuesday and Thursday.

C **Practice Exercise B with two partners.**

▶ READING CHALLENGE 1

A Write.

1. What time is your English class? My English class is at _________________.
2. What time is lunch? Lunch is at _________________.

B Read.

C Write.

1. What time is work? ______*7:00 A.M.*______
2. What time is lunch? ____________________
3. What time is English class? ____________________
4. What time is dinner? ____________________

▶ VOCABULARY CHALLENGE

A Read.

B Read to a partner and point.

1. Shiro sits *next to* Julie.
2. The students are *in* the classroom.
3. The paper is *on* the desk.
4. The trashcan is *between* the bookcase and the desk.
5. The file cabinets are *in the corner*.
6. The clock is *on* the wall.

Circle.

1. The books are in / next to the bookcase.

2. The board is in / between the clock and the flag.

3. Julie sits next to / on Shiro.

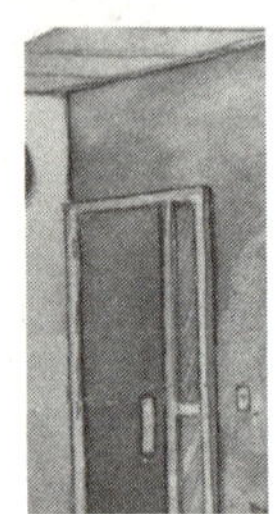

4. The door is in / next to the corner.

D Look at the picture on page 15. Write.

There **is** a . . .
There **is** one . . .

There **are** two . . .
There **are** three . . .

1. There are two f _ _ _ c _ _ _ _ _ _ _ .
2. There are two c _ _ _ _ _ _ _ _ .
3. There is a c _ _ _ _ .
4. There are five s _ _ _ _ _ _ _.

▶ READING CHALLENGE 2

▶ PRE-READING

A **Read.**

First name: Irma
Last name: Perez
Age: 47 years old
Marital status: Married
Birthplace: Mexico
Phone: (202) 555-7769
School: Fort Lauderdale Adult

B **Answer the questions.**

1. Where is Irma from? She is from ________________.
2. Where does she go to school? She goes to ______________________________.

C **Read about Irma's classroom.**

Classroom inventory	
Number	**Item**
30	student desks
10	computers
1	file cabinet

D **Practice with a partner.**

A: How many desks are in Irma's classroom?

B: There are 30 desks.

▶ READING

E **Read Irma's story.**

My Classroom

I'm Irma Perez. I'm from Guadalajara, Mexico. I go to Fort Lauderdale Adult School. I go to school on Monday and Wednesday at 11:00 A.M. My classroom is big. There are 30 desks. There is one file cabinet next to the board. There is one bookcase in my classroom. I sit next to Olivia.

F **Read Choi's story.**

Choi's Classroom

This is Choi Soon Young. He is from Seoul, Korea. He goes to Fort Lauderdale Adult School. He goes to school on Tuesday and Thursday at 5:00 P.M. His classroom is small. There are 11 desks. There are two windows, two clocks, and five computers. He sits next to Binh.

► COMPREHENSION

G **Write.**

Classroom inventory	
Number	**Item**
	student desks
	computers

H **Answer the questions.**

1. What time is English class for Irma? ______________________
2. What time is English class for Choi? ______________________

I Write.

1. Her name is ______________________.
2. She is from ______________________.
3. She goes to ______________________.
4. Her classroom is ______________________ (big, small).
5. There are ______________________ desks.
6. She sits next to ______________________.

J Write.

1. His name is ______________________.
2. He is from ______________________.
3. He goes to ______________________.
4. His classroom is ______________________ (big, small).
5. There are ______________________ desks.
6. He sits next to ______________________.

► EXTENSION

K Write about your classroom.

1. Where do you go to school? ______________________
2. Who do you sit next to? ______________________

▶ WRITING CHALLENGE

▶ PREPARING

A **Write.**

My classroom inventory	
Number	**Item**
	student desks
	computers
	file cabinet
	boards
	clocks
	trashcans
	doors
	windows
	bookcase
	flag

B **Write about your classroom.**

1. There are ______________________________ desks.
2. There is a ______________________________.
3. The board is next to ______________________________.
4. ______________________________
5. ______________________________
6. ______________________________

C Answer questions.

1. What is your name?

   My name is ______________________________.

2. Where are you from?

   I'm from ______________________________.

3. Where do you go to school?

   I go to ______________________________.

4. Is your classroom big or small?

   My classroom is ______________________________.

5. What time is your English class?

   My English class is at ______________________________.

6. Who do you sit next to?

   I sit next to ______________________________.

D Circle (a) or (b).

1. Who do you sit next to?

   a. i sit next to andrea.

   (b.) I sit next to Andrea.

2. How many desks are in your classroom?

   a. There are 20 desks.

   b. there are 20 desks.

3. Where is the file cabinet?

   a. The file cabinet is in the corner

   b. The file cabinet is in the corner.

▶ WRITING

E **Write about your classroom.**

My Classroom

I'm ____________. I'm from ____________.

I go to ____________. My English class is at ____________. My classroom is ____________. There are ______ desks. There ____________ in my classroom. I sit next to ____________.

F **Write the paragraph again.**

My Classroom

▶ EDITING

G **Check your writing.**

- Capital letters: My name is James. ~~my~~ name is ~~j~~ames.
- Periods: I am from Argentina.

H **Check a partner's writing.**

- Capital letters: My name is James. ~~my~~ name is ~~j~~ames.
- Periods: I am from Argentina.

I **Rewrite your paragraph on another sheet of paper.**

▶ Community Challenge

Write about schools in your community.

1. School name: ______________________

   Address: ______________________

2. School name: ______________________

   Address: ______________________

3. School name: ______________________

   Address: ______________________

UNIT 3 Food

▶ GETTING READY

A **Look at the picture.**

B **Read.**

Augustin: What is for dinner?

Silvia: I don't know. What do you want?

Augustin: I want chicken. What do you want?

Silvia: I want chicken, too.

Augustin: OK. But we don't have any chicken!

Silvia: Let's add it to the shopping list.

C **Practice Exercise B with a partner.**

▶ READING CHALLENGE 1

A **Write.**

1. What do you want for dinner?

____

2. What do you want for dessert?

____

B **Read.**

C **Draw a line from the picture to the word.**

▶ VOCABULARY CHALLENGE

A **Read.**

chicken

chicken sandwich and fruit

hamburger and fries

taco and chips

vegetables and rice

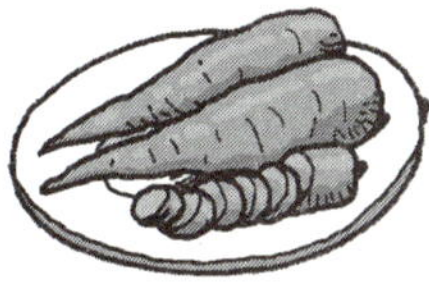
carrots

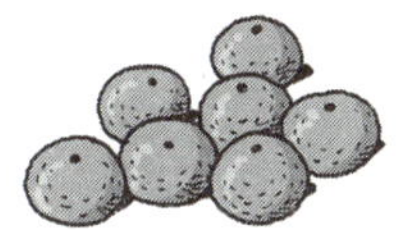
oranges

apples

chips

cookies

milk

water

cake

pie

ice cream

sundae

chocolate

candy

B **Read to a partner and point.**

C Write.

Dinner	Snack	Dessert
chicken	*carrots*	*cookies*

D Write.

I **like** . . .	I **eat** . . .	I **love** . . .
He **likes** . . . She **likes** . . .	He **eats** . . . She **eats** . . .	He **loves** . . . She **loves** . . .

1. When I am hungry, I eat  a *s* _ _ _ _ _ _ _ _.

2. She likes 

c _ _ _ _ for a snack.

3. She eats  *o* _ _ _ _ _ _ _ and 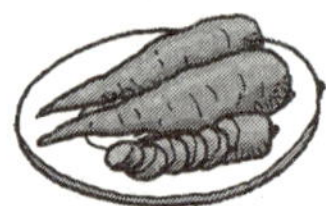

c _ _ _ _ _ _ _ for snacks.

4. I like  *v* _ _ _ _ _ _ _ _ _ and *r* _ _ _ for dinner.

5. Maria loves  *i* _ _ *c* _ _ _ _ for dessert.

6. I eat  *c* _ _ _ _ _ _ for dinner.

▶ READING CHALLENGE 2

▶ PRE-READING

A **Read.**

First name: Ron
Last name: Carter
Age: 52 years old
Marital status: Married
Birthplace: Texas
Phone: (777) 555-3220
School: Fair Oaks Adult, Texas

B **Answer the questions.**

1. Where does Ron live? He lives in ______________________.
2. How old is he? He is ________ ________ ________.

C **Read Ron's shopping list.**

Shopping List
bread
potatoes
oil
lettuce
tomatoes
rice
vegetables

▶ READING

D **Read about Ron.**

The Food I Eat

My name is Ron Carter. I like hamburgers and fries. I eat cookies and chips for snacks. I also love ice cream and chocolate for dessert. This is the food I eat.

E **Read Christine's story.**

The Food Christine Eats

This is Christine Brideau. She likes to eat many different things. She likes chicken sandwiches and fruit. She eats fruits and vegetables for snacks. She also loves fruits for dessert. This is the food she likes.

▶ COMPREHENSION

F Write the information.

Meal	Meal
hamburgers and fries	
Dessert	**Dessert**
Snack	**Snack**

G Write.

1. Ron eats ______________________________ for dinner.
2. Ron ______________________________ for dessert.
3. Ron ______________________________ for snacks.
4. Christine ______________________________ for dinner.
5. Christine ______________________________ for dessert.
6. Christine ______________________________ for snacks.

H Make a shopping list for Christine.

Shopping List

chicken

______

______

______

______

______

______

I Answer the questions.

1. What does Ron like for dessert?

______

2. What does Christine like for dessert?

______

► EXTENSION

J Practice with a partner.

A: What do you like for dinner?

B: I like chicken for dinner.

▶ WRITING CHALLENGE

▶ PREPARING

A **What do you like? Write.**

Dinner	Dessert	Snacks

B **Write about food you like.**

1. I like ____________________ for dinner.
2. I love ____________________ ________ ____________.
3. I eat ____________________ ________ ____________.
4. I like ____________________ for dessert.
5. I love ____________________ ________ ____________.
6. I eat ____________________ ________ ____________.
7. I like ____________________ for snacks.
8. I love ____________________ ________ ____________.
9. I eat ____________________ ________ ____________.

C **Make a shopping list for today.**

Shopping list	

D Ask a partner questions.

1. What is your name?

   His/Her name is ______________________________.

2. What do you like for dinner?

   He/She likes ______________________________.

3. What do you like for snacks?

   ____

4. What do you like for dessert?

   ____

E Circle (a) or (b).

1. What does Emilio like for dinner?
   a. He likes tacos chips for dinner.
   b. He likes tacos and chips for dinner.
2. What does Francesca like for dessert?
   a. she likes cookies and chocolate for dessert.
   b. She likes cookies and chocolate for dessert.
3. What does Andre like for a snack?
   a. He like carrots for a snack.
   b. He likes carrots for a snack.
4. What does Janet eat for a snack?
   a. She eats chips
   b. She eats chips.

► WRITING

F **Write about a partner.**

The Food ____________ Eats

____________ likes to eat many different things. ________ likes ______________________. ________ eats ____________ for snacks. ________ loves ____________ for dessert. This is the food ________ likes.

G **Write the paragraph again.**

▶ EDITING

H **Check your writing.**

- Capital letters: My name is James. ~~m~~y name is ~~j~~ames.
- Periods: I am from Argentina.

I **Check a partner's writing.**

- Capital letters: My name is James. ~~m~~y name is ~~j~~ames.
- Periods: I am from Argentina.

J **Rewrite your paragraph on another sheet of paper.**

▶ Community Challenge

Plan a party at your home for twenty people. Make a shopping list.

Shopping list

Clothing

▶ GETTING READY

A **Look at the picture.**

B **Read.**

Salesperson: Can I help you?

Ivan: I want to buy this pair of shoes.

Salesperson: OK, one pair of shoes. That's $34.50.

Ivan: This is a very big store.

Salesperson: Yes, sir. Can I help you find anything else?

Ivan: No, thanks. One pair of shoes is all I want today.

C **Practice Exercise B with a partner.**

▶ READING CHALLENGE 1

A **Write.**

1. Do you have a checking account? ______________________

2. Do you have a checkbook? ______________________

B **Read.**

IVAN BORICOV
8233 HENDERSON STREET
NEW YORK CITY, NY 10012

1025

DATE: March 13, 2005

PAY TO THE ORDER OF Adel's Clothing Emporium $ 34.50

thirty-four and 50/100 DOLLARS

NATIONBANK

MEMO Shoes

Ivan Boricov

⑆0009345 AB876543 /01025

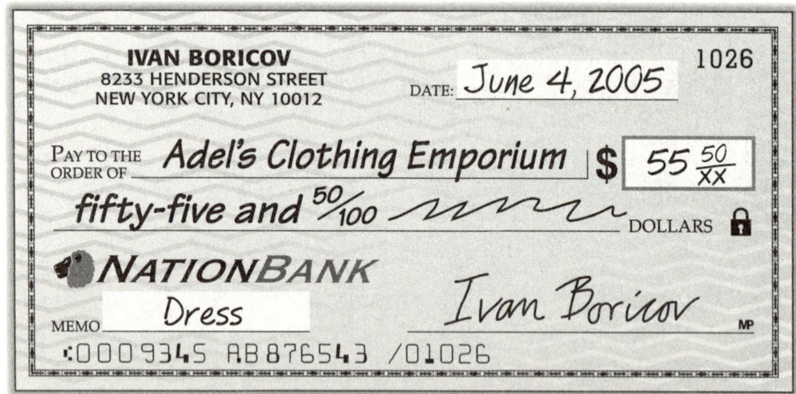
IVAN BORICOV
8233 HENDERSON STREET
NEW YORK CITY, NY 10012

1026

DATE: June 4, 2005

PAY TO THE ORDER OF Adel's Clothing Emporium $ 55 50/XX

fifty-five and 50/100 DOLLARS

NATIONBANK

MEMO Dress

Ivan Boricov

⑆0009345 AB876543 /01026

C **Answer the questions.**

1. How much is check 1025 for? $ ______________________

2. How much is check 1026 for? $ ______________________

3. What is check 1025 for? ______________________

4. What is check 1026 for? ______________________

▶ VOCABULARY CHALLENGE

A Read.

1. jeans
2. tennis shoes
3. pants
4. ties
5. shirts
6. jackets
7. sweaters
8. pajamas
9. socks
10. coats
11. raincoats
12. hats
13. skirts
14. sneakers
15. pants
16. blouses
17. shirts
18. dresses
19. shoes

B Read to a partner and point.

C Write.

The blouse **is** $34.00.
The blouses **are** $34.00 each.

1. The  *b* _ _ _ _ _ _ _ _ are $34.00 each.

2. The  *s* _ _ _ _ _ is $25.00.

3. The  *s* _ _ _ _ _ are $5.00 each.

4. The  *c* _ _ _ _ _ are $60.00 each.

D Write.

Men's clothes	Women's clothes
ties	*blouse*

E Write.

1.  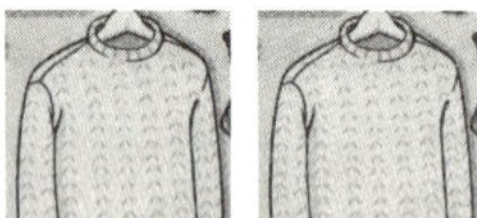     

I have *three sweaters*, ________________, and ________________ in my closet.

2.     

I have ________________, ________________ pairs of ________________, and ________________ in my closet.

▶ READING CHALLENGE 2

▶ PRE-READING

A **Read the advertisement.**

B **Circle.**

1. Adel's has clothes for men. Yes No
2. Adel's has clothes for women. Yes No

C **Write.**

1. How much are the sweaters?

   The sweaters are ____________________.

2. How much are the blouses?

   The blouses are ____________________.

3. How much are the dresses?

   The dresses are ____________________.

D **Read about Adel's Clothing Emporium.**

Adel's Clothing Emporium

I go to Adel's Clothing Emporium for clothes. It is a big store. The clothes are for men and women. John is the manager and Arlene is a salesperson. There are blouses, dresses, shoes, and sweaters. The shirts are $22.50. I like Adel's Clothing Emporium.

E **Read about J.D. Allen's Clothing Store.**

J.D. Allen's Clothing

This is J.D. Allen's Clothing Store. It is a small store. The clothes are for men and women. There are shoes, shirts, pants, and coats. The shirts are on sale this week. They are $14.00. This is a good store.

► COMPREHENSION

F Write the information.

~~small store~~	women's and men's	Shirts are $22.50
big store	Shirts are on sale.	Shirts are $14.

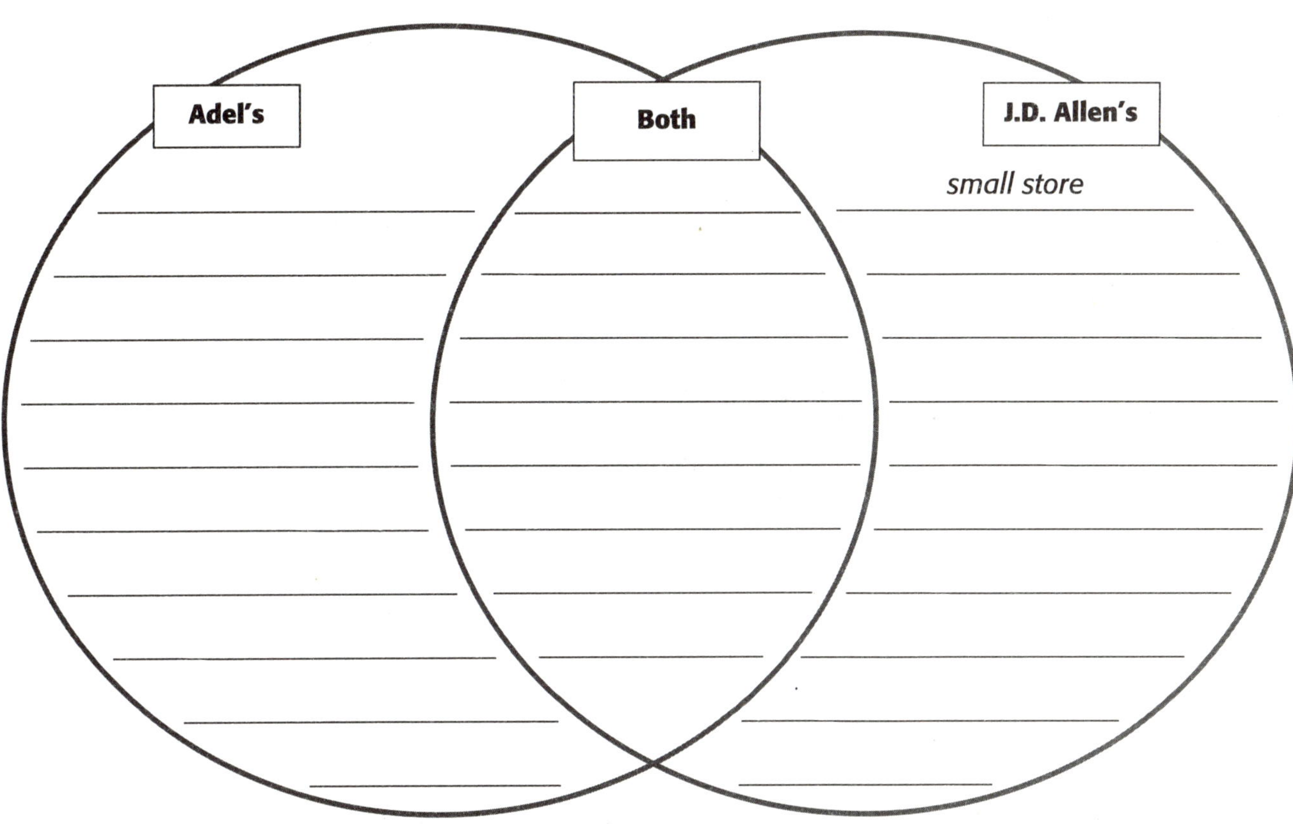

G Answer the questions.

1. Who is the manager at Adel's Clothing Emporium?

   His name is ______________________________.

2. Who is the salesperson?

   Her name is ______________________________.

3. Is J.D. Allen's a big store?

   ____

H **Write.**

1. (Store name) ____________________
2. (Size: big/small) ____________________
3. (Clothes) ____

____

I **Write.**

1. (Store name) ____________________
2. (Size: big/small) ____________________
3. (Clothes) ____

____

▶ EXTENSION

J **Practice with a partner.**

A: How much are the blouses at Adel's?

B: They are $18.00.

▶ WRITING CHALLENGE

▶ PREPARING

A **Write the names of three clothing stores in your community.**

1. ______________________________
2. ______________________________
3. ______________________________

B **Choose one store. Write.**

Name	
Address	
Size	☐ big store ☐ small store
Clothes	☐ men's clothes ☐ women's clothes ☐ pants ☐ shirts ☐ blouses ☐ sweaters ☐ socks ☐ coats ☐ hats ☐ shorts ☐ dresses ☐ jeans ☐ skirts ☐ shoes ☐ __________ ☐ __________ ☐ __________ ☐ __________

C Write.

1. The store name is ______________________________.

2. The address is ______________________________.

3. The store is ________________ (big, small).

4. There are ________________, ________________, and ________________.

D What clothes do you want? Make a list.

Clothing

E Circle (a) or (b).

1. What clothes do you like at Adel's?

   a. I like the shoes, dresses, and blouses.

   b. I like the shoes dresses and blouses.

2. How much are the blouses?

   a. The blouses are $65.00.

   b. The blouses is $65.00.

3. What clothes are there in the store?

   a. There is shoes, socks, and pants.

   b. There are shoes, socks, and pants.

▶ WRITING

F **Write about a clothing store in your community.**

____

I like ____________ Clothing Store. The address ____________ ________. It is a ____________ store. The clothes are for ____________. ____________________. There are ________, ________, and ________. ________ ________ are $________. I like ____________.

G **Write the paragraph again.**

▶ EDITING

H **Check your writing.**

- Capital letters: My name is James. ~~my~~ name is ~~j~~ames.
- Periods: I am from Argentina.

I **Check a partner's writing.**

- Capital letters: My name is James. ~~my~~ name is ~~j~~ames.
- Periods: I am from Argentina.

J **Rewrite your paragraph on another sheet of paper.**

▶ Community Challenge

Find two clothing stores in your community. Complete the charts.

Clothing store name	
Address	
Do they have men's, women's, or all clothes?	
What's on sale?	

Clothing store name	
Address	
Do they have men's, women's, or all clothes?	
What's on sale?	

UNIT 5 Our Community

▶ GETTING READY

A **Look at the picture.**

B **Read.**

Adriano: Hello, Isaac?

Isaac: Yes, this is Isaac.

Adriano: This is Adriano. I'm lost.

Isaac: Where are you going?

Adriano: Can you give me directions to Food Mart?

Isaac: Yes, where are you now?

Adriano: I'm on First Street next to National Bank.

Isaac: Oh, it's nearby. Go straight on First and turn right on Anaheim Street.

C **Practice Exercise B with a partner.**

▶ READING CHALLENGE 1

A Write.

1. I live in (town/city name) ________________.
2. I live in a (house, apartment, mobile home, or condominium) ________________.

B Read.

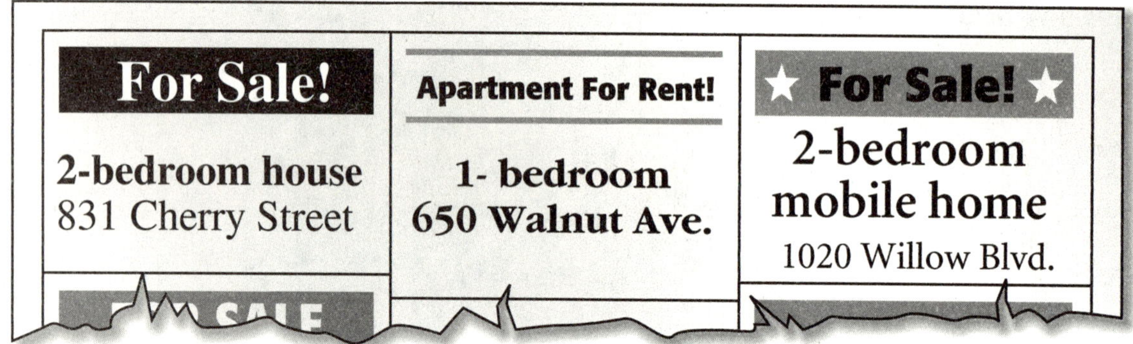

C Answer the questions.

1. How many bedrooms does the house have?

   ____

2. How many bedrooms does the apartment have?

   ____

3. How many bedrooms does the mobile home have?

   ____

VOCABULARY CHALLENGE

A **Read.**

supermarket

pharmacy

hospital

bank

car

train

bus

bicycle

Turn left.

Turn right.

Go straight.

Stop.

B **Read to a partner and point.**

C Write.

I **live** in Santa Ana.
We **drive** to school.
You **ride** to school.
They **walk** to school.

He **takes** the bus.
She **rides** to school.

1. I take the  ____________________ to school.

2. They take a  ____________________ to work every day.

3. She drives a  ____________________ to work.

4. Mario rides his  ____________________ to school.

D Write.

Places	Transportation	Directions
supermarket	*car*	*stop*

E Read the map.

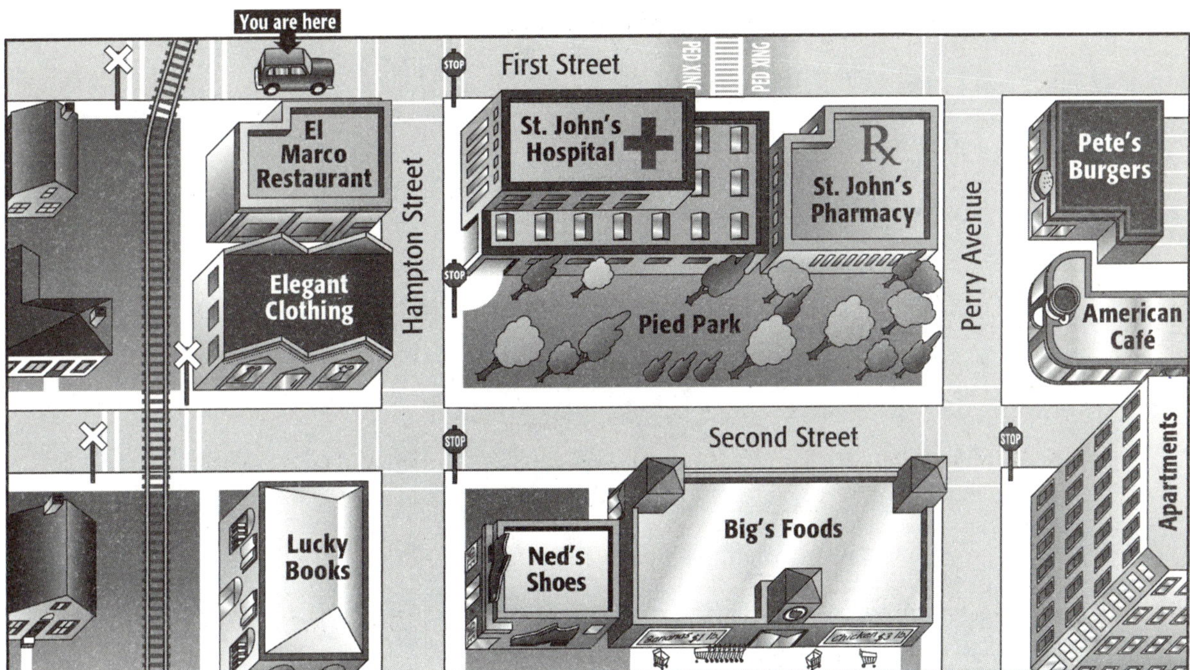

F Read the directions. Circle (a), (b), or (c).

1. Go straight on First Street. Turn right on Hampton. It's next to the park.
   a. the restaurant
   b. the hotel
   c. the hospital
2. Go straight on First Street. Turn right on Hampton. Turn left on Second. It's next to Ned's Shoes.
   a. Big's Foods
   b. the apartments
   c. Lucky Boots
3. Go straight on First Street. Turn right on Perry Avenue. Stop at ________.
   a. the park
   b. the pharmacy
   c. the apartments

READING CHALLENGE 2

PRE-READING

A **Write the words.**

New York City	Mexico City
Washington Adult School	apartment
bicycle	4435 Washington Ave.
Mario	Marshall Street

Name	
Birthplace	
City	*New York City*
Home street	
Home	
Transportation	
School	
School address	

▶ READING

B **Read about Mario.**

My Community

My name is Mario. I'm from Mexico. I live in New York City. I live on Marshall Street. I live in an apartment next to a pharmacy. I go to Washington Adult School. I ride my bicycle to school every day. I go straight on Marshall and turn right on Washington. The address is 4435 Washington Avenue. It's next to the supermarket.

C **Read about Anya.**

Anya's Community

This is Anya. She is from Russia. She lives in New York City. She lives on Second Street. She lives in an apartment next to other houses. She goes to Pendleton School. She drives to school every day. The address is 2900 Bradford. She goes three miles on Second Street, turns left on Michelson, and then she turns right on Bradford. The school is next to a park.

► COMPREHENSION

D **Write about Anya.**

Name	
Birthplace	
City	
Home street	
Home	
Transportation	
School	
School address	

E **Write.**

1. Where is Washington Adult School?

____

2. Where is Pendleton School?

____

3. Where is Mario from?

____

4. Where is Anya from?

____

F Complete the chart.

drives a car to school	rides a bike to school
lives in an apartment	lives in New York City
is from Russia	is from Mexico

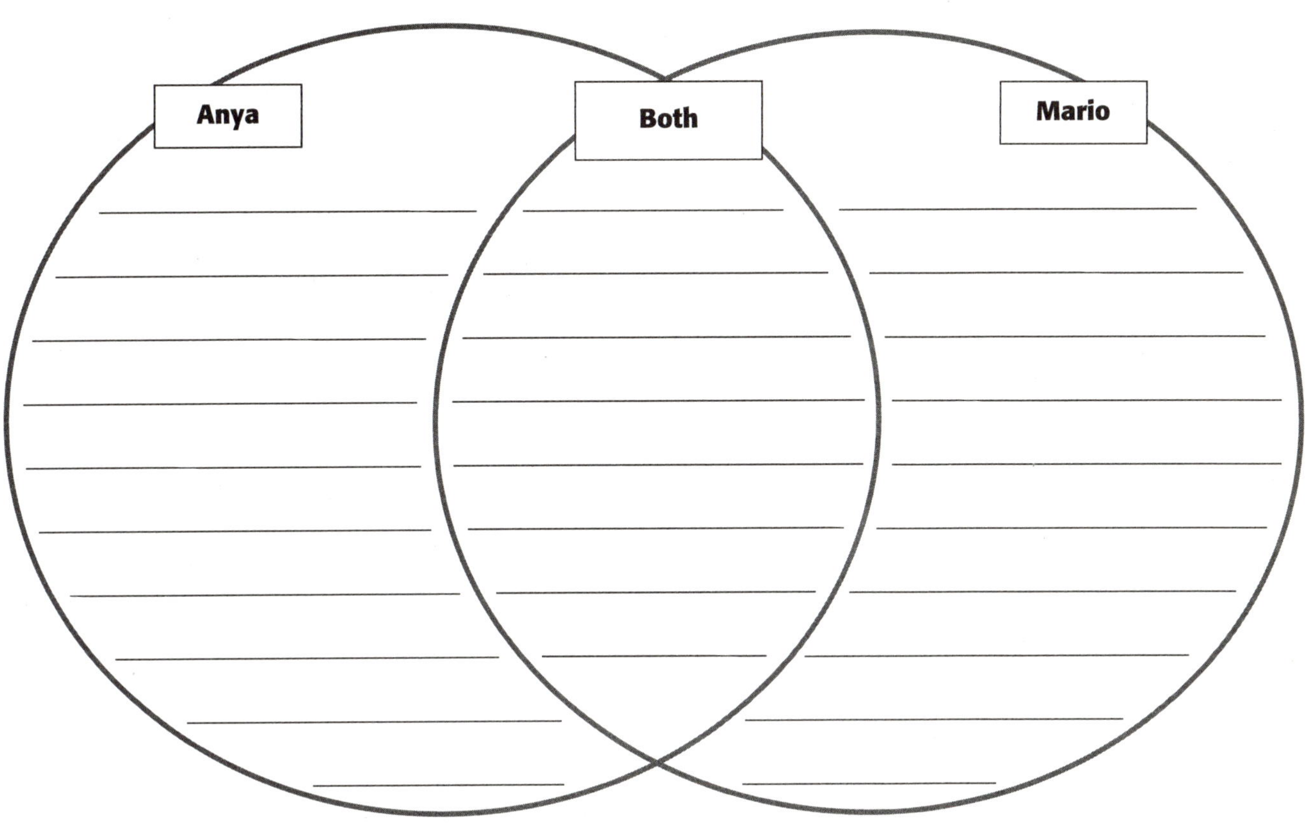

► EXTENSION

G Practice with a partner.

A: Who lives in an apartment?

B: Mario.

▶ WRITING CHALLENGE

▶ PREPARING

A **Write about you.**

Name	1.
Birthplace	2.
City	3.
Home street	4.
Home	5.
Transportation	6.
School	7.
School address	8.

B **Write about Exercise A.**

1. My name is ____________________.
2. I am from ____________________.
3. I live in ____________________.
4. I live on ____________________.
5. I live in ____________________.
6. I ____________________ to school.
7. I go to ____________________.
8. The address is ____________________.

C **Answer the questions.**

1. What is next to your home?

   ____________________ is next to my home.

2. What is next to your school?

   The school is next to ____________________.

▶ WRITING

D **Write about your community.**

My Community

My name ________________. I'm ________. I live ________________. I live in ________________ next to ________________. I go to ________________ ________________. I ________________ to school every day. The address is ________________. It's next to ________________. I study English in school.

E **Write the paragraph again.**

▶ EDITING

F **Check your writing.**

- Capital letters: My name is James. ~~my~~ name is ~~j~~ames.
- Periods: I am from Argentina.

G **Check a partner's writing.**

- Capital letters: My name is James. ~~my~~ name is ~~j~~ames.
- Periods: I am from Argentina.

H **Rewrite your paragraph on another sheet of paper.**

▶ Community Challenge

A **Find out about someone in your community.**

Name	
Birthplace	
City	
Home street	
Home	
Transportation	
School	
School address	

B **Tell your class about the person.**

Healthy Living

▶ GETTING READY

A **Look at the picture.**

B **Read.**

Nurse: Hello, Doctor Nadir's office. Can I help you?

Alexi: Yes, I want to make an appointment.

Nurse: OK. What's the matter?

Alexi: I have a terrible headache and a stomachache.

Nurse: Please come in at 3:00 today. Is that OK?

Alexi: Yes, thank you. I will come at 3:00.

C **Practice Exercise B with a partner.**

▶ READING CHALLENGE 1

A **Check (✓).**

1. Do you get a checkup every year?

☐ Yes ☐ No

2. How many times a year do you see a doctor?

☐ once a year ☐ twice a year ☐ other: ______________

B **Read.**

January 25, 2006

Name	Time	Problem	Phone
Chinh Tran	2:15	checkup	555-1235
Elsa Kusmin	3:00	headache	555-5842
Orlando Ramirez	3:45	leg hurts	555-3765
Amal Jahshan	4:30	backache	555-2220
Fawzia Ahadi	5:15	cold	555-9876

C **Answer the questions.**

1. Who has a checkup? ______________
2. What is Fawzia's problem? ______________
3. What time is the appointment for Elsa? ______________
4. What is Orlando's phone number? ______________

▶ VOCABULARY CHALLENGE

A **Read.**

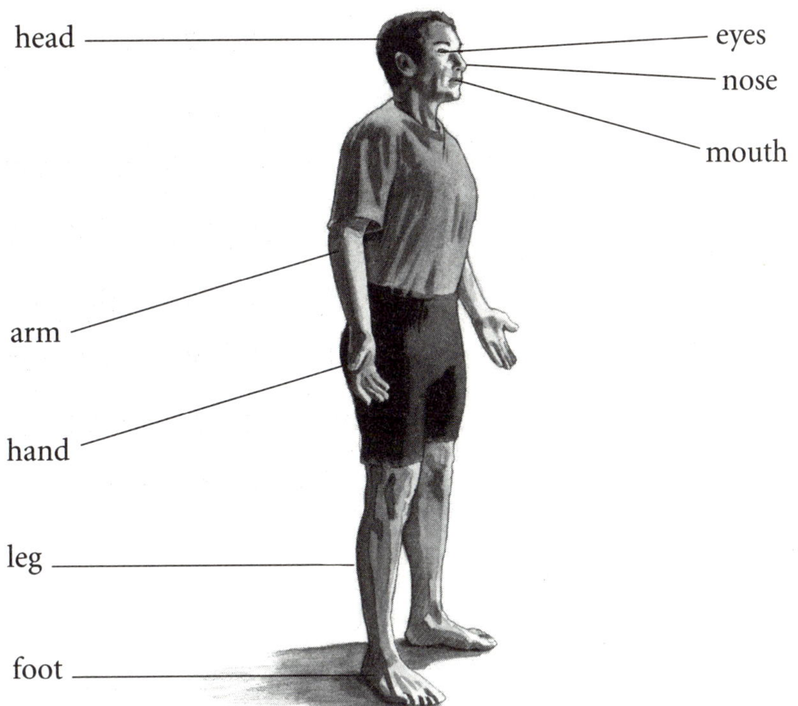

Sleep eight hours.

Get a ***checkup*** once a year.

Exercise every day.

Eat three meals every day.

Don't ***smoke***.

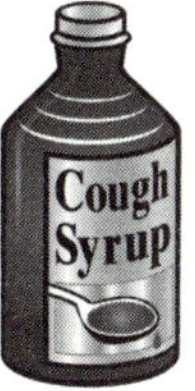

Take your ***medicine***.

B **Read to a partner and point.**

C Write.

My leg hurts.
Your leg hurts.
His leg hurts.
Her leg hurts.

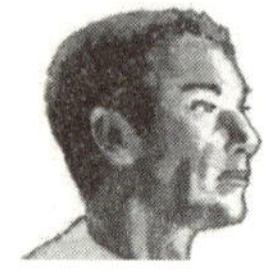

1. My __________ hurts.

2. My __________ hurts.

3. Her __________ hurts.

4. Ayumi's __________ hurts.

D Circle (a), (b), or (c).

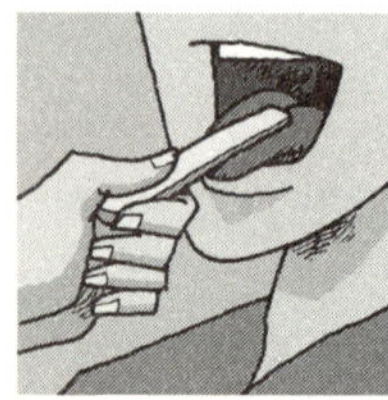

1. Please open your______________.
   a. mouth
   b. leg
   c. nose

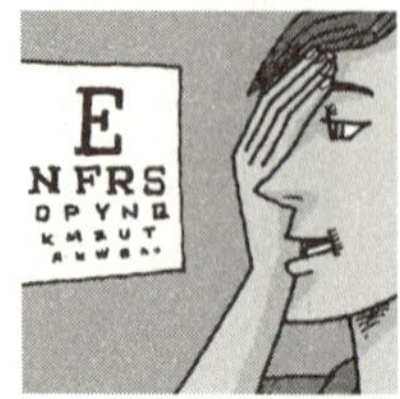

2. My ______________ hurts.
   a. ears
   b. back
   c. eye

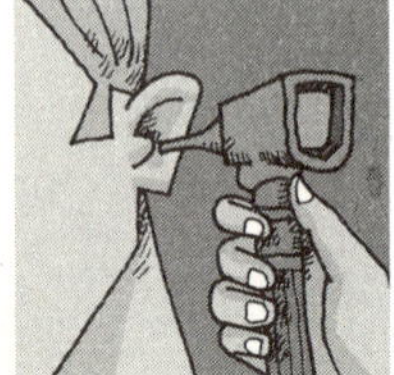

3. Let me look in your ______________.
   a. stomach
   b. ear
   c. leg

E Write.

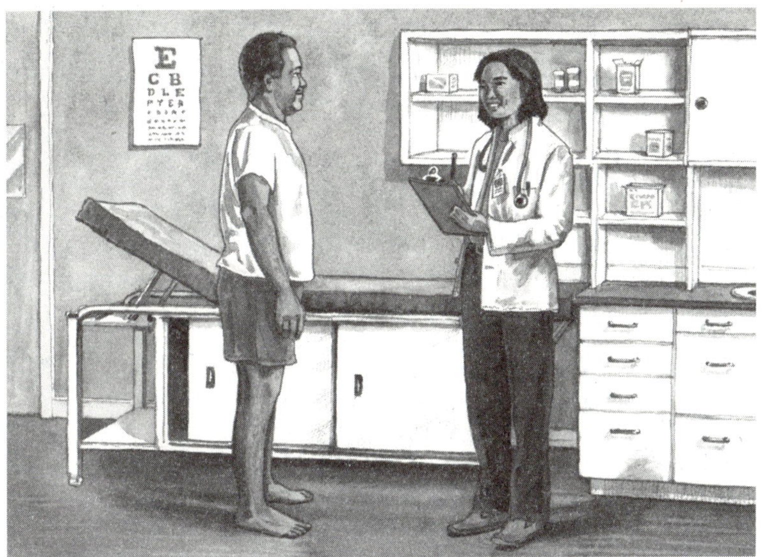

Doctor: Do you s _ _ _ _?

Guillermo: No, I don't.

Doctor: Do you e _ _ _ _ _ _ _?

Guillermo: Yes, I do.

Doctor: Do you s _ _ _ _ eight hours a day?

Guillermo: Yes, I do.

Doctor: Do you e _ _ three good meals every day?

Guillermo: Yes, I do.

Doctor: You are very healthy!

▶ READING CHALLENGE 2

▶ PRE-READING

A **Write the information in the chart.**

~~Hasna~~	once a year
0 minutes a day	six hours a day
lunch and dinner	no

Name	*Hasna*
Sleep	
Meals	
Exercise	
Checkup	
Smoke	

B **Circle *good, bad,* or *OK* health.**

Name	*Lien*
Sleep	*3 hours a day*
Meals	*2 meals*
Exercise	*no*
Checkup	*no*
Smoke	*yes*

good / bad / OK

Name	*Marie*
Sleep	*6 hours a day*
Meals	*3 meals*
Exercise	*10 minutes*
Checkup	*no*
Smoke	*no*

good / bad / OK

Name	*Gilberto*
Sleep	*8 hours a day*
Meals	*3 meals*
Exercise	*30 minutes*
Checkup	*once a year*
Smoke	*no*

good / bad / OK

READING

C **Read about Julia and her health.**

My Health

My name is Julia. I am forty years old and single. I sleep eight hours a day. I eat breakfast, lunch, and dinner. I exercise thirty minutes every day. I don't smoke. I get a checkup once a year. I think I am in good health.

D **Read about Dalmar and his health.**

Dalmar's Health

This is Dalmar. He is twenty-seven years old and married. He smokes. He doesn't get a checkup every year. He sleeps five hours a day. He eats breakfast, lunch, and dinner. He exercises twenty minutes a day. Dalmar is unhealthy.

▶ COMPREHENSION

E **Write the information about Dalmar.**

Name	*Dalmar*
Sleep	
Meals	
Exercise	
Checkup	
Smoke	

F **Circle *Yes* or *No*.**

1. Dalmar doesn't smoke.	Yes	No
2. Julia eats breakfast.	Yes	No
3. Dalmar sleeps eight hours a day.	Yes	No
4. Julia doesn't exercise.	Yes	No
5. Dalmar doesn't go to the doctor.	Yes	No
6. Dalmar and Julia eat breakfast.	Yes	No

I **don't** exercise.
They **don't** exercise.

Julia **doesn't** exercise.
Dalmar **doesn't** exercise.

Write information in the chart.

sleeps 8 hours a day	gets a checkup once a year
exercises	eat breakfast, lunch, dinner
sleeps 5 hours a day	is in good health
smokes	is unhealthy

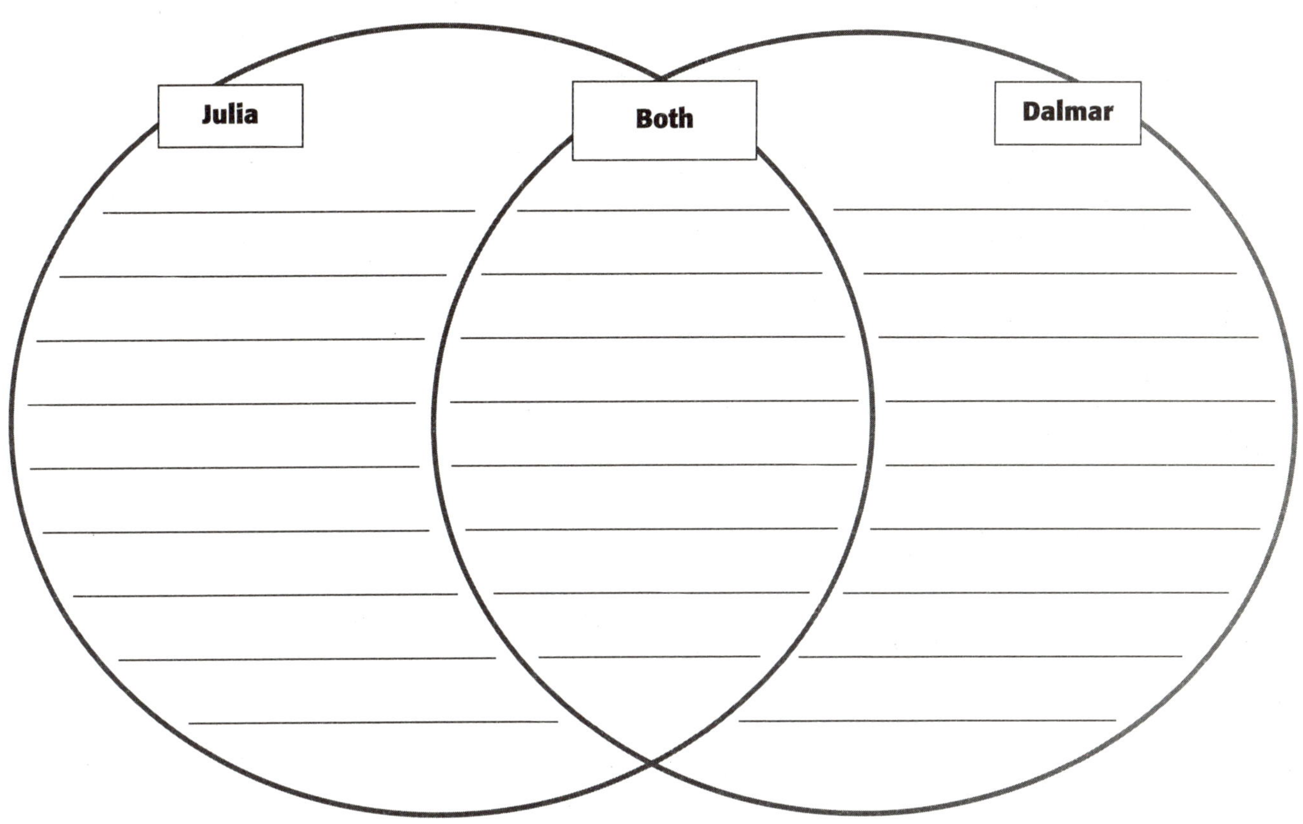

▶ EXTENSION

Practice

A: Who sleeps eight hours?

B: Julia sleeps eight hours.

WRITING CHALLENGE

PREPARING

A **Write about you.**

Name	1.
Sleep	2.
Meals	3.
Exercise	4.
Checkup	5.
Smoke	6.

B **Write about Exercise A.**

1. My name is ______________________________.
2. I sleep ______________________________.
3. ______________________________
4. ______________________________
5. ______________________________
6. ______________________________

C **Circle (a), (b), or (c).**

I am in __________ health.

a. good

b. OK

c. bad

▶ WRITING

D **Write about your health. See page 67 for samples.**

	My Health	

▶ EDITING

E **Check your writing.**

- Capital letters: My name is James. ~~m~~y name is ~~j~~ames.
- Periods: I am from Argentina.

F **Check a partner's writing.**

- Capital letters: My name is James. ~~m~~y name is ~~j~~ames.
- Periods: I am from Argentina.

G **Rewrite your paragraph on another sheet of paper.**

A Find out about someone in your community.

Name	1.
Sleep	2.
Meals	3.
Exercise	4.
Checkup	5.
Smoke	6.

B Write about the person.

C Tell your class about the person.

Work

▶ GETTING READY

A **Look at the picture.**

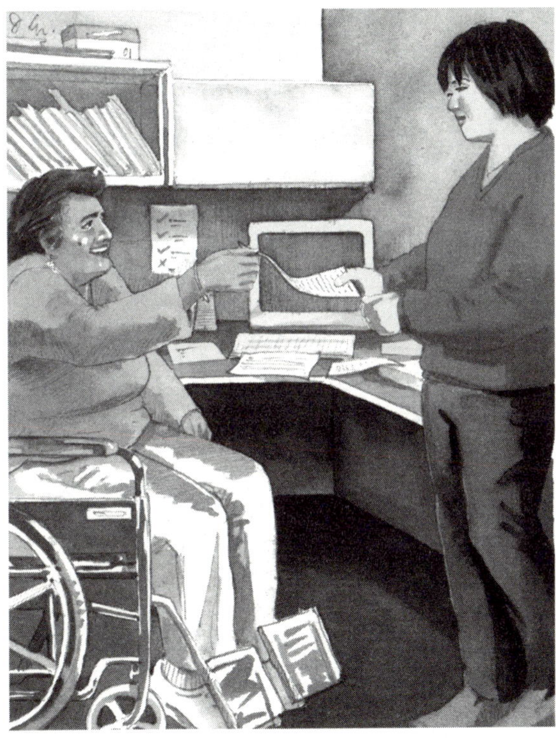

B **Read.**

Manager: Miyuki, I have a new job for you.

Miyuki: On the computer?

Manager: Yes, that's right, on the computer. It's easy.

Miyuki: I can type very well on a computer.

Manager: Good! You can type letters here on this computer.

C **Practice Exercise B with a partner.**

▶ READING CHALLENGE 1

A **Write.**

1. Do you work? ____________
2. Are you a good worker? ____________

B **Read.**

NATIONAL SALES CORPORATION

Employee Evaluation Form

Name:	*Amy Ochoa*	
Position:	*Receptionist*	
Date:	*June 27, 2005*	
Helps customers	(Yes)	No
Comes to work on time	(Yes)	No
Speaks English well	(Yes)	No
Follows directions well	(Yes)	No
Supervisor:	*Kenny Gomez*	

C **Answer the questions.**

1. What is the name of Amy's supervisor? ________________________
2. Does Amy follow directions? ________________________
3. What is the date? ________________________

VOCABULARY CHALLENGE

A **Read.**

A ***cashier*** works in a supermarket.

A ***teacher*** works in a school.

A ***receptionist*** answers the phones.

A ***bus driver*** drives a bus.

A ***custodian*** mops floors.

A ***student*** studies in school.

A ***manager*** works in a store.

A ***salesperson*** talks to customers.

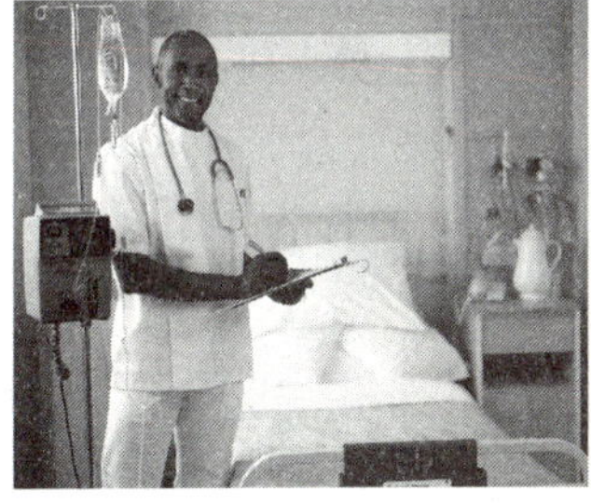

A ***nurse*** works in a hospital.

B **Practice with a partner.**

A: What does a custodian do?

B: A custodian mops floors.

C Write.

I **answer** phones.
He **answers** phones.

1. Pedro **is** a ______________________________.
   He ______________________________ floors.

2. Jessica ______________________________.
   She ______________________________.

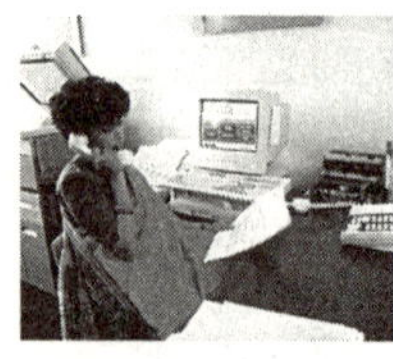

3. Amy ______________________________.
   She ______________________________.

4. Chen ______________________________.
   He ______________________________.

5. Hanif ______________________________.
   He ______________________________.

6. John ______________________________.
   He ______________________________.

7. Emilio ______________________________.
   He ______________________________.

D Match.

1. A salesperson —— b.
2. A student
3. A teacher
4. A cashier
5. A nurse
6. A manager

a. works in a school.
b. talks to customers.
c. works in a supermarket.
d. works in a hospital.
e. studies in school.
f. works in an office.

E Write the sentences from Exercise D.

1. *A salesperson talks to customers.*
2. ______________________________
3. ______________________________
4. ______________________________
5. ______________________________
6. ______________________________

F Write.

School	Business	Other
teacher		*bus driver*

READING CHALLENGE 2

PRE-READING

A **Look at the planner.**

A.M. = in the morning

12:00 P.M. to 5:59 P.M. = in the afternoon

After 6:00 P.M. = at night

B **Answer the questions.**

1. When does Amy start work?

____

2. When does she take a lunch break?

____

3. When does she go home?

____

4. How many hours does she work?

____

▶ READING

C **Read about Amy.**

My Job

My name is Amy. I am a receptionist for a company in San Francisco. I like my job. I work from 9:00 in the morning to 5:00 in the afternoon. My supervisor is Kenny. I answer phones and speak to customers. I work very hard. I have a great job.

D **Read about Pedro.**

Pedro's Job

Pedro is a custodian for a company in San Francisco. He doesn't like his job. He works from 10:00 P.M. to 7:00 A.M. every night. Pedro works alone. He doesn't have a supervisor at night. He takes a short break at midnight and at 4:00 A.M. His lunch break is at 2:00 A.M. He mops the floors and takes out the trash. He comes to work on time, and he works very hard. Pedro likes people, and doesn't like to work alone.

▶ COMPREHENSION

E **Write the information about Pedro in the planner.**

Monday Evening	
4:30 P.M.	
5:00 P.M.	
5:30 P.M.	
6:00 P.M.	
6:30 P.M.	
7:00 P.M.	
7:30 P.M.	
8:00 P.M.	
8:30 P.M.	
9:00 P.M.	
9:30 P.M.	
10:00 P.M.	
10:30 P.M.	
11:00 P.M.	
11:30 P.M.	
12:00 A.M.	

Tuesday Morning	
12:30 A.M.	
1:00 A.M.	
1:30 A.M.	
2:00 A.M.	
2:30 A.M.	
3:00 A.M.	
3:30 A.M.	
4:00 A.M.	
4:30 A.M.	
5:00 A.M.	
5:30 A.M.	
6:00 A.M.	
6:30 A.M.	
7:00 A.M.	
7:30 A.M.	
8:00 A.M.	

F **Answer the questions.**

1. Does Pedro like his job? ____________________
2. Does Amy like her job? ____________________
3. When does Pedro start work? ____________________
4. When does Amy start work? ____________________
5. How many hours does Pedro work? ____________________
6. How many hours does Amy work? ____________________

G Write information in the chart.

Name: ______	Name: ______
City: ______	City: ______
Job: ______	Job: ______
Duties: ______	Duties: ______
Supervisor: ______	Supervisor: ______
Start work: ______	Start work: ______
Go home: ______	Go home: ______

▶ EXTENSION

H Practice with a partner. Ask the questions.

1. What are Pedro's/Amy's duties?
2. Who is Pedro's/Amy's supervisor?
3. What is the name of Pedro's/Amy's job?
4. When does Pedro/Amy start work?
5. When does Pedro/Amy go home?

▶ WRITING CHALLENGE

▶ PREPARING

A **Write about you.**

Work
1. Name: ______________________
2. City: ______________________
3. Job: ______________________
4. Duties: ______________________
5. Supervisor: ______________________
6. Start work: ______________________
7. Go home: ______________________

OR

School
1. Name: ______________________
2. City: ______________________
3. Job: ______________________
4. Duties: ______________________
5. Teacher: ______________________
6. Start school: ______________________
7. Go home: ______________________

B **Write about Exercise A.**

1. My name is ______________________________.
2. I live in ______________________________.
3. ______________________________
4. ______________________________
5. ______________________________
6. ______________________________
7. ______________________________

C **Circle.**

1. I like / don't like my job / school.
2. I like / don't like my supervisor / teacher.

▶ WRITING

D **Write about your job or school. See page 79 for samples.**

	My Job	

▶ EDITING

E **Check your writing.**

- Capital letters: My name is James. ~~m~~y name is ~~j~~ames.
- Periods: I am from Argentina.

F **Check a partner's writing.**

- Capital letters: My name is James. ~~m~~y name is ~~j~~ames.
- Periods: I am from Argentina.

G **Rewrite your paragraph on another sheet of paper.**

A **Talk to people in the community. Complete the survey.**

Name: ______ City: ______ Job: ______ Duties: ______ Supervisor: ______ Start work: ______ Go home: ______	Name: ______ City: ______ Job: ______ Duties: ______ Supervisor: ______ Start work: ______ Go home: ______
Name: ______ City: ______ Job: ______ Duties: ______ Supervisor: ______ Start work: ______ Go home: ______	Name: ______ City: ______ Job: ______ Duties: ______ Supervisor: ______ Start work: ______ Go home: ______

B **Report your findings to your class.**

Lifelong Learning and Review

▶ GETTING READY

A **Look at the picture.**

B **Read.**

Lien: Hello, Mario.

Mario: Hello, Lien.

Lien: I need to speak good English.

Mario: Why?

Lien: I want to go to college.

Mario: I want to learn English, too. I want a good job.

Lien: Do you want to study together?

Mario: That's a great idea!

C **Practice Exercise B with a partner.**

READING CHALLENGE 1

A **Write**

1. Why do you want to learn English? ______________________
2. Do you have goals for the future? ______________________

B **Read.**

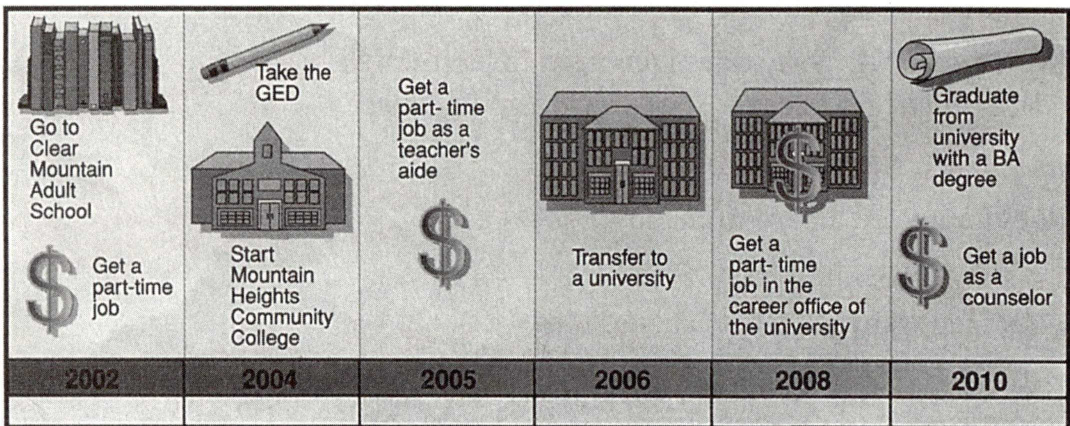

C **Answer the questions.**

1. What does Lien want to do in 2002?

   She wants to get ______________________.

2. What does Lien want to do in 2005?

   She wants to ______________________.

3. What does Lien want to do in 2008?

   She wants to ______________________.

4. What does she want to do in 2010?

   She wants to ______________________.

VOCABULARY CHALLENGE

A Read.

I ***organize*** my homework in a portfolio.

Nubar ***studies*** English every day.

Hernandez can ***ask*** questions in a store.

I can ***give directions.***

I can ***fill in*** a form.

Edgar can ***join in*** class activities.

Concepcion ***listens*** to tapes.

Raquel can ***write*** in English.

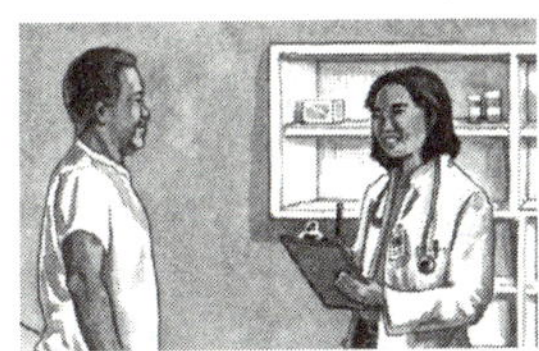

Guillermo can ***tell*** the doctor what's wrong.

Consuela and Ricardo can ***discuss*** problems with their neighbors.

Emilio can ***follow instructions.***

She can ***buy*** clothes in a store.

B Practice with a partner.

A: What can you do?

B: I can give directions.

C Write.

1. I ____________ to my teacher.
2. I ____________ to audio tapes to learn English.
3. Raul ____________ English every day.
4. They ____________ lots of questions.
5. She ____________ ____________ all the classroom activities.

D Match.

1. I can buy	a. to her house.
2. I can fill in	b. at work.
3. He can follow directions	c. an application form.
4. I can organize	d. clothes.
5. She can give directions	e. his doctor what's wrong.
6. Mario can tell	f. my binder.

E Write the sentences from Exercise D.

1. *I can buy clothes.*
2. ____
3. ____
4. ____
5. ____
6. ____

▶ READING CHALLENGE 2

▶ PRE-READING

Read the schedule.

ALI'S SCHEDULE

	Sunday	Monday	Tuesday	Wednesday	Thursday	Friday	Saturday
6:00 A.M.							
9:00 A.M.		*School*		*School*		*School*	
11:00 A.M.							
1:00 P.M.		*Works*	*Works*	*Works*	*Works*	*Works*	
3:00 P.M.							
5:00 P.M.	*Dinner*	*Dinner*	*Dinner*	*Dinner*	*Dinner*	*Dinner*	*Dinner*
7:00 P.M.	*Studies*	*Studies*	*Studies*	*Studies*	*Studies*	*Studies*	

B **Answer the questions.**

1. When does Ali study at school?
   Ali studies on Monday, Wednesday, and Friday.
2. When does he work?
   ____
3. When does he study at home?
   ____
4. When does he have dinner?
   ____
5. Does he go to school on Saturday?
   ____

▶ READING

C **Read about Ali and Marie.**

About Me

My name is Ali. I'm from Nigeria. I go to Arthur Adult School in Chicago. I study English in school on Monday, Wednesday, and Friday. I study English at home every day. I study two hours a day at home. I organize my work in my binder. I can speak a little English. I can buy things at the store. I can give and follow directions. I want to learn English. I want to go to college.

About Me

My name is Marie. I am from Haiti. I go to Clear Mountain Adult School in Los Angeles. I study English in school on Tuesdays and Thursdays. I study English at home every day. I study an hour a day at home. I write in a notebook. I can speak English quite well. I can discuss problems with my neighbors. I can tell my doctor what's wrong. I can talk about my personal life to others. I want to learn English. I want to be a nurse.

▶ COMPREHENSION

D Write the information about Ali.

Name	
Birthplace	
City	
School	

E Write sentences. What can Ali do?

1. He can ______________________________.
2. ______________________________.
3. ______________________________.
4. ______________________________.

F Write the information about Marie.

Name	
Birthplace	
City	
School	

G Write sentences. What can Marie do?

1. She can ____________________.
2. ____________________
3. ____________________
4. ____________________

H Answer the questions.

1. What does Ali want?
   He wants to ____________________
   ____
2. What does Marie want to be?
   ____
   ____

▶ EXTENSION

I Practice with a partner. Ask the questions.

1. What can Ali do?
2. What can Marie do?
3. What does Ali want?
4. What does Marie want?

▶ WRITING CHALLENGE

▶ PREPARING

A **What can you do? Write sentences.**

1. I can ______________________________________.
2. ______________________________________
3. ______________________________________
4. ______________________________________

B **Fill in your schedule.**

MY SCHEDULE

	Sunday	Monday	Tuesday	Wednesday	Thursday	Friday	Saturday

C **Write.**

1. I want to ______________________________________.
2. ______________________________________

▶ WRITING

D **Write about things you can do.**

▶ EDITING

E **Check your writing.**

- Capital letters: My name is James. ~~m~~y name is ~~j~~ames.
- Periods: I am from Argentina.

F **Check a partner's writing.**

- Capital letters: My name is James. ~~m~~y name is ~~j~~ames.
- Periods: I am from Argentina.

G **Rewrite your paragraph on another sheet of paper.**

Talk to people in the community. Complete the surveys.

Name: ______________________

What are three goals you have?

1. ______________________
2. ______________________
3. ______________________

Name: ______________________

What are three goals you have?

1. ______________________
2. ______________________
3. ______________________

Name: ______________________

What are three goals you have?

1. ______________________
2. ______________________
3. ______________________

APPENDIX

VOCABULARY LIST

Unit 1
first name
last name
years old
married
divorced
single
birthplace
from
school

Unit 2
window
flag
file cabinets
computers
board
clock
wall
bookcase
books
door
plant
paper
trashcan
next to
in
on
between
in the corner

Unit 3
chicken
sandwich
fruit
hamburger
fries
taco
vegetables
rice
carrots
oranges
apples
chips
cookies
milk
water
cake
pie
ice cream
sundae
chocolate
candy

Unit 4
jeans
tennis shoes
pants
ties
shirts
jackets
sweaters
pajamas
socks
coats
raincoats
hats
skirts
sneakers
pants
blouses
shirts
dresses
shoes

Unit 5
supermarket
pharmacy
hospital
bank
car
train
bus
bicycle
turn left
turn right
go straight
stop

Unit 6
head
eyes
nose
mouth
arm
hand
leg
foot
sleep
checkup
exercise
eat
smoke
medicine

Unit 7
cashier
teacher
receptionist
bus driver
custodian
student
manager
salesperson
nurse

Unit 8
organize
study
ask
give directions
fill in
join in
listen
write
tell
discuss
follow instructions
buy

IRREGULAR VERB FORMS

be	was	**hear**	heard
become	became	**hide**	hid
begin	began	**hit**	hit
blow	blew	**keep**	kept
break	broke	**know**	knew
bring	brought	**lead**	led
build	built	**leave**	left
buy	bought	**lose**	lost
catch	caught	**make**	made
choose	chose	**meet**	met
come	came	**pay**	paid
cut	cut	**put**	put
do	did	**run**	ran
drink	drank	**say**	said
drive	drove	**see**	saw
eat	ate	**send**	sent
fall	fell	**sleep**	slept
feel	felt	**speak**	spoke
fight	fought	**spend**	spent
find	found	**take**	took
fly	flew	**teach**	taught
forget	forgot	**tell**	told
get	got	**think**	thought
give	gave	**understand**	understood
go	went	**wear**	wore
grow	grew	**win**	won
have	had	**write**	wrote

▶ USEFUL WORDS

Cardinal numbers

1	one
2	two
3	three
4	four
5	five
6	six
7	seven
8	eight
9	nine
10	ten
11	eleven
12	twelve
13	thirteen
14	fourteen
15	fifteen
16	sixteen
17	seventeen
18	eighteen
19	nineteen
20	twenty
21	twenty-one
30	thirty
40	forty
50	fifty
60	sixty
70	seventy
80	eighty
90	ninety
100	one hundred
1000	one thousand
10,000	ten thousand
100,000	one hundred thousand
1,000,000	one million

Ordinal numbers

first	1st
second	2nd
third	3rd
fourth	4th
fifth	5th
sixth	6th
seventh	7th
eighth	8th
ninth	9th
tenth	10th
eleventh	11th
twelfth	12th
thirteenth	13th
fourteenth	14th
fifteenth	15th
sixteenth	16th
seventeenth	17th
eighteenth	18th
nineteenth	19th
twentieth	20th
twenty-first	21st

Days of the week

Sunday
Monday
Tuesday
Wednesday
Thursday
Friday
Saturday

Seasons

winter
spring
summer
fall

Months of the year

January
February
March
April
May
June
July
August
September
October
November
December

Write the date

April 5, 2004 = 4/ 5/ 04

Temperature chart

Degrees Celsius (°C) and
Degrees Fahrenheit (°F)

°C	°F
100°C	212°F
30°C	86°F
25°C	77°F
20°C	68°F
15°C	59°F
10°C	50°F
5°C	41°F
0°C	32°F
–5°C	23°F

Weights and measures

Weight:
1 pound (lb.) = 453.6 grams (g)
16 ounces (oz.) = 1 pound (lb.)
1 pound (lb.) = .45 kilogram (kg)

Liquid or Volume:
1 cup (c.) = .24 liter (l)
2 cups (c.) = 1 pint (pt.)
2 pints = 1 quart (qt.)
4 quarts = 1 gallon (gal.)
1 gallon (gal.) = 3.78 liters (l)

Length:
1 inch (in. or ″) = 2.54 centimeters (cm)
1 foot (ft. or ′) = .3048 meters (m)
12 inches (12″) = 1 foot (1′)
1 yard (yd.) = 3 feet (3′) or 0.9144 meters (m)
1 mile (mi.) = 1609.34 meters (m) or 1.609 kilometers (km)

Time:
60 seconds = 1 minute
60 minutes = 1 hour
24 hours = 1 day
28–31 days = 1 month
12 months = 1 year

MAP OF THE UNITED STATES

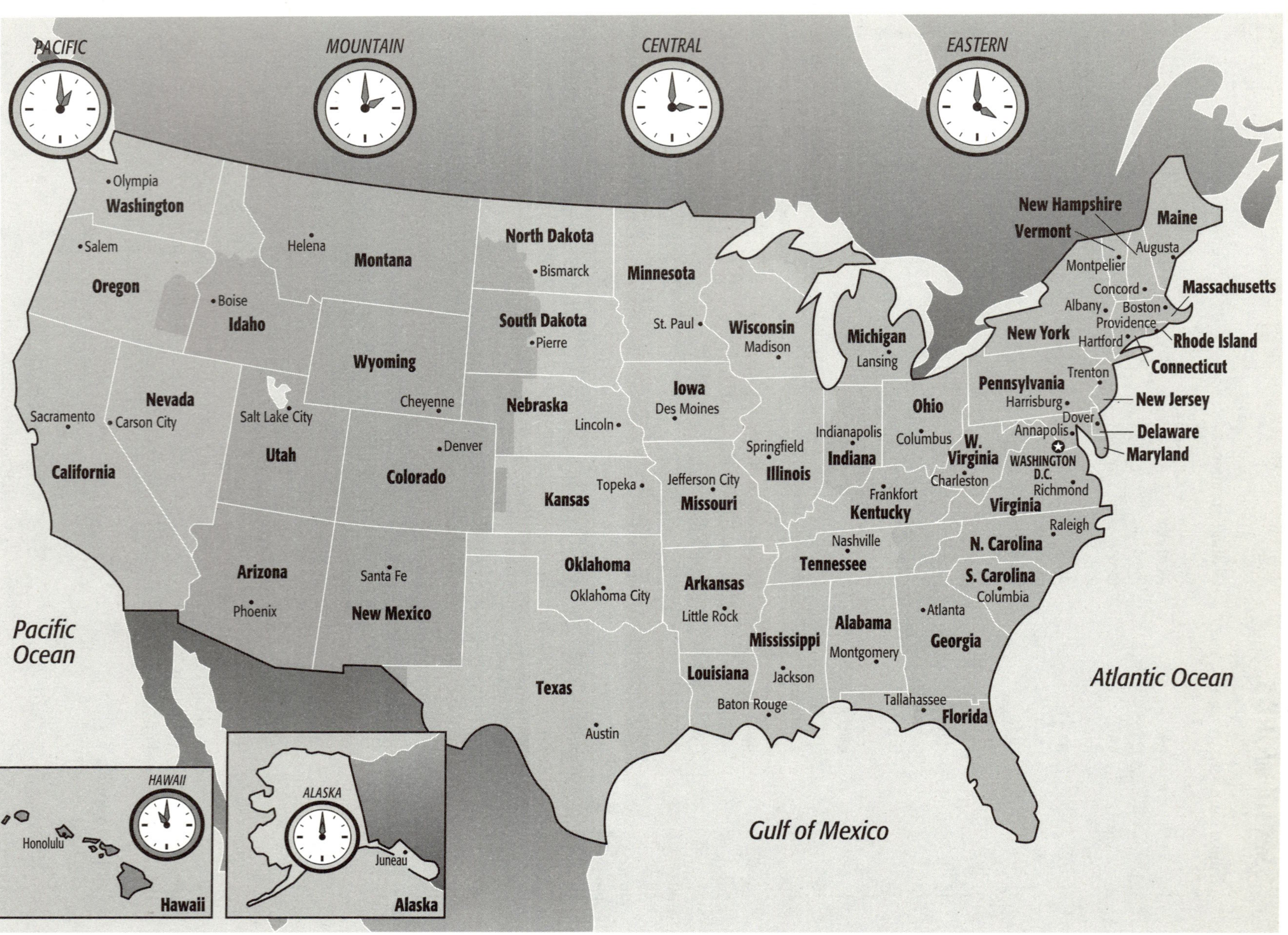